. . . FOR THIS LITTLE BOOK

"How I wish I'd had *The Little Book of Meditation* when I first tried to learn to meditate! It's so clear, so real, so practical. Dr. Bear has done us all a great service with her writing and teaching skills to make such a valuable tool as meditation available to us."
—**Charles T. Tart, Ph.D.**
Author: *States of Consciousness, Transpersonal Psychologies, Living the Mindful Life*, and many other books.
Professor Emeritus of Psychology, University of California

"I highly recommend this little treasure of a book on meditation. It is practical, witty, and humorous. It is written for the nonspecialist, for anyone wishing to learn exercises that will improve the quality of their lives. Based on the vast experience of the author's work as a teacher and a learner, it provides us with a variety of common sense approaches to meditation. It's easy to read, and fun—like having a little talk with a new friend."
—**Steven D. Goodman, Ph.D.**
Professor, California Institute for Integral Studies
Author: *Transforming the Causes of Suffering*

"This book on meditation is a treasure trove of insights and inspiration. The writing is clear and accessible; the writer, Dr. Bear, is knowledgeable and wise. If you're interested in learning how to train your mind towards wisdom and compassion, this is the book for you. You'll receive plenty of guidance and support from Dr. Bear, who has been practicing and teaching meditation for many years. I highly recommend this book."
—**Ronna Kabatznick, Ph.D.**
Former Psychologist to Weight Watchers International
Author: *The Zen of Eating*
Founder, Mindful Management, Berkeley

*All men's miseries derive from not being able
to sit in a quiet room alone.*
—BLAISE PASCAL

THE LITTLE BOOK

OF MEDITATION

A Guide to
Stress-Free Living

MARINA C. BEAR, Ph.D.

SLG BOOKS
BERKELEY & HONG KONG

First published in 2010 by
SLG Books
P. O. Box 9465 • Berkeley, California 94709
www.slgbooks.com • info@slgbooks.com

© 2010 by Marina C. Bear
Illustrations © 2010 by Marina C. Bear
Wood blocks © 2000 and 2010 by Roger Willians
Cover photograph © iStockPhoto.com/RollingEarth

First Paperback Edition
Printed in the United States of America

This edition is printed on acid-free paper that meets the
American National Standards Institute Z39.48 Standard.

Distributed by Publishers Group West,
a member of the Perseus Books Group

Library of Congress Cataloging-in-Publication Data

Bear, Marina, 1941-
The little book of meditation : a guide to stress-free living / Marina C. Bear.
    p. cm.
Includes bibliographical references and index.
ISBN 978-0-943389-41-7 (alk. paper)
1. Meditation. 2. Stress (Psychology) I. Title.
BF637.M4B43 2010
158.1'2--dc22
                                2009031904

10 9 8 7 6 5 4 3 2 1

A GUIDE TO THE BOOK

INTRODUCTION

Ready, Set, Stop!

You've read it in the media:
+ A movie star meditates every day to keep her sanity in the crazy busy world of Hollywood.
+ Hospitals everywhere are offering classes in meditation to help patients lower their blood pressure and cope with chronic pain.
+ Psychotherapists affirm that patients who learn to meditate deal with anger and stress more easily.

But did you also know that:
+ People with skin disorders experience four times the cure rate when they meditate during treatment.
+ Professional sports coaches recommend meditation to develop focus and clarity under pressure . . . and quarterbacks who meditate complete more passes.
+ Regular meditation can counteract the effects of aging on the brain.

From the moment our feet hit the floor in the morning, we're not only doing something, we're simultaneously thinking about the next thing.

When you try to stop and reflect on what you just did, another demand crops up. Sometimes it seems the faster you run, the further behind you get. You can't possibly process all the information coming at you from all directions.

Is there hope? There is. People all over the globe have found that they can:

* have a positive effect on their health in a way that doesn't involve exercise or giving up dessert,
* increase their efficiency at work,
* manage their stress, tension, and the increasing demands of their jobs, and
* actually expand their capacity to enjoy life

simply by taking a few minutes every day to just . . . stop.

We're often exhausted, but all too often the ways we try to relax end up adding to our burdens. Somebody says, "Join a gym. The exercise will loosen you up." But you resent the time it takes to get there and when you don't get there, you feel guilty about the money you're spending not exercising. When you're supposed to be enjoying a vacation, doing nothing but relaxing, you keep fretting about the pile of things you'll need to do when you get home, not to mention the cost of the vacation and what the kids are up to.

Does any of this apply to you? If so, then you may be ready to try the classic meditators' advice: Don't just do something—sit there! With a few simple instructions and some suggestions and encouragement, you can make this powerful method of recharging your mental and physical batteries a part of your day.

So what is meditation, anyway?

You've got a mind and body and a life. Meditation is a way to help the first two function at their best—which goes a long way toward improving your life. Through meditation you can learn to:

* calm your mind (and ease your body),
* deal with stressful situations,
* manage pain rather than letting it manage you,
* enjoy your life a lot more (and really notice that you're enjoying it!),
* use and enjoy your talents to their fullest, and
* meet the curve balls life throws at you with a better perspective and maybe even a sense of humor.

The best part is that you can do all this and more by simply taking a few minutes a day to just let yourself be.

Okay, that sounds a little vague. But for centuries people have used meditation for these and other benefits. And during that long history, they've developed methods and techniques that make it possible for anyone to reach a state of evenness and calm, relaxation and awareness. All you have to do is be willing to try.

There's a reason why meditation is often referred to as "sitting." That's what it is at the most basic level. But it's actually a whole lot more.

What meditation *isn't* is some strange practice you do in an uncomfortable position for a long time that involves stopping all your thoughts or joining a cult. And it's definitely not a waste of time.

In fact, although you may associate meditation with Eastern religions, it's basically a human thing. Anybody with a body and a brain can do it and benefit from it. Of course many of the books and manuals that offer training in meditation come from religious traditions. This book is different. All it presumes is that if you're still reading at this point, you're open to the possibility that you could be happier, more efficient, calmer, and healthier.

This book was written primarily for people who are curious about meditation, but who aren't prepared to take on a whole belief system to learn it. If you have a religious or spiritual path already, meditation can support you on that journey. If you aren't interested in religion, meditation will still be a source of knowledge on a personal level.

I've been practicing one form of meditation or other all my adult life. I've taught it to many people who signed up for meditation courses, and I've snuck it into my curriculum when teaching college classes in world religions. Why? To me, it seems essential that, as a teacher, I make the idea of religious or spiritual practice real to students who may not have had any kind of religious training.

Students tell me that they use these simple techniques in any number of settings where they feel the need of a little tranquility and a fresh approach to things. I firmly believe that a more peaceful world is a better world, and that the capacity to create that world resides in every one of us. The more of us there are living lives with self-awareness and joy the less road rage and international chaos we'll have to deal with.

What you hold in your hand is a brief but complete guide to beginning meditation. It starts with basic information, defining meditation and some of the words people use to talk about it. Why it's a good idea. Some of the fascinating scientific findings about the effects of meditation on the brain (they're all good!). There's practical advice on how to begin, including tips for physical comfort and suggestions to keep you motivated. As you begin to make meditation a part of your regular routine, you'll find suggestions for other ways to make use of it in your daily life.

As with any endeavor, there will be times when the smooth pebbles in the stream seem to turn into boulders in the road. Challenges can come from many directions, but there are ways to meet them and well-tested routes around those boulders.

Learning to meditate is one of the best gifts you can give yourself. It will be useful for the rest of your life. When times are going really well, it can keep you grounded and fully aware of your good fortune without losing the sense of your place in the rest of the world. In grief or adversity it can help keep you from becoming overwhelmed by despair. Your friends and family will notice a change in your outlook and your ability to respond to their needs and concerns.

As it turns out, meditation is a gift you give the rest of us, too. I hope this little book will give you an excellent start.

*Twenty years from now you will be
more disappointed by the things you didn't do
than by the ones you did do.*

—MARK TWAIN

THE
BASICS

JUST SIT THERE?

Meditation is a way of being—being present right here, in this moment, knowing who you are and being comfortable with yourself.

Mostly, we're surrounded by distractions. You can call it entertainment, or passing the time, but too often the messages being beamed your way include more than a little discomfort. There's good stuff you're supposed to want—do you have enough of it? Do you look the way you're supposed to? Are you having all the fun you're entitled to? Have you done everything on your list? And if not, what can we sell you to make it faster and easier?

Okay, so now what's the alternative?

It's simple. You're in charge. By turning away from the endless chatter, you'll find a basic you that's stable, confident, and comfortable.

Meditation is not a way of making your mind quiet.
It's a way of entering into the quiet that's already there—
buried under the 50,000 thoughts
the average person thinks every day.
—DEEPAK CHOPRA

You can think of meditation as a way of training or taming your mind. It's a process and it takes some time, but it's worth it. Once you know how to find that place of quiet stability, you can cope. A calm, focused approach will get you out of a difficult situation—whether it's a burning building or an angry boss—more reliably than a state of panic or anger. Worry becomes optional: Shall I worry about something I can't do anything about, or shall I take a hike, clean my desk, or practice the tuba? Faced with a challenging problem, beating your head against it frequently turns into just repeating the situation over and over in your mind. Having something else to do with your mind at times like that is a good thing.

Meditation is a different way of using your mind. It's both fascinating and rewarding. It's a way of discovering abilities you didn't know you had that are not only interesting, but useful in every aspect of your life.

Meditation helps increase your ability to pay attention. It ups your level of awareness. The things that bring you joy become more enjoyable. You see the things that cause you pain but, because you can meet problems without the added hot sauce of fear, rage, or the need to hide, your chance of resolving painful situations is a lot better.

So what do we do? Just sit there? Hold on. We've said a little about what meditation is. Let's take a few moments to say what meditation isn't.

WHAT MEDITATION IS NOT

Meditation isn't the property of any single religion or tradition. All over the world, in desert huts, on mountain tops, on round cushions and park benches, there are people engaged in meditation. All the major world religions have some form of meditative practice. In fact, a lot of what we know about the history and the development of various meditative techniques comes from those religious traditions.

But you don't have to belong to a religion or hold any particular religious beliefs to learn to practice meditation. It turns out that meditation is a basic human thing. If you've got a mind and a body, you can meditate.

Meditation is not a fancy word for daydreaming. Daydreaming, spacing out, and drifting around in inner space can be relaxing, but they're not meditation. Mostly, they're escape routes from reality, and when you get back from your "time out," your worries and problems will still be there, waiting for you.

There is not one perfect way to do meditation. Although sitting in a particular posture, burning incense, repeating certain words, or looking at a special object can have a place in your meditation, they're just a collection of ways into meditation. They can support you once you're there, too, but they're techniques, not the actual thing. And just doing those things while letting your mind ramble through your favorite fantasy or skitter from one problem to another isn't meditation either. If you sat down to meditate and you stand up more tired and fuzzy-minded at the end of the session, it wasn't meditation.

Finally, meditation isn't some heavy-handed brakeman you hire to stop your thoughts. And it isn't some kind of super mind control that will change your whole inner landscape. It's more about relaxing and allowing than forcing anything. You start with who you are, what you've got, and where you find yourself. What can change is your attitude towards those things, from frustration and dissatisfaction to acceptance and a clearer sense of where change is possible.

Occasionally, somebody asks me if meditation can be dangerous. Given a world in which you can kill yourself by drinking too much water, I'd have to say that human beings can make anything dangerous. Meditation isn't a substitute for psychiatric care when someone is seriously off the tracks, but for most of us mildly neurotic souls, it's only a benefit.

What lies behind us and lies before us are small matters
compared to what lies within us.
—RALPH WALDO EMERSON

PRAYER, CONTEMPLATION,
AND MEDITATION

Prayer, contemplation, and meditation may seem quite similar. And, in fact, they share certain characteristics. The difference is in the focus and the goal of the practice rather than what it looks like from the outside.

There are lots of different kinds of prayer, but in most traditions the focus is outside of yourself. You're addressing a higher power and asking for help or forgiveness, or offering praise or thanks. If you're hoping for an answer to your prayer, you probably have to quiet down and listen. Calming your mind is one of the first stages of meditation, so learning to meditate can have a positive effect on your efforts at prayer.

Prayer tends to be active—you are talking to an outside entity, asking for something or expressing something. By comparison, contemplation is usually a quiet reflection on something—an idea, an object, a process. In contemplation, you may be holding something in your mind and gently looking at it from all sides. When people say they have to contemplate a

22

situation, that's the kind they usually mean. There's a deeper kind of contemplation, though. In a religious sense, contemplation means to enter into a kind of spiritual awareness of relationship to whatever you know to be the source of the sacred. You don't have to do anything with that awareness. You just inhabit it.

In meditation, by comparison, you're developing the capacity to manage your mind. You direct your attention inward rather than outward. To help develop the ability to stay with that redirected attention rather than following the thoughts and feelings that are sure to crop up, you may use an object to anchor your vision or a sound to hold your mind, but those are just techniques that many find useful. Meditation is a way of being that emerges from the calm and clarity of your mind when it's not captured by outside input or negative emotions. It's learned in as supportive a situation as you can arrange, and ultimately it illuminates the rest of your life.

Prayer is when you talk to God;
meditation is when you listen to God.
—DIANA ROBINSON

WHY DO IT?

Whatever its cause, stress is a central part of life in the 21st century. Jobs, relationships, the state of the economy and the world in general, and even our compulsion to excel in the things we do for recreation all add up. Stress takes its toll on your health, your outlook, and your general well-being. If only there were a simple solution. In fact, there is.

A regular practice of meditation can lower your blood pressure and help you cope with any physical and psychic pains that come your way. Rather than being a victim of worry and anxiety, through meditation you discover the way to a place of calm and clarity from which to deal with whatever comes along. As your natural mindfulness develops, simple pleasures take on new meaning and your natural sense of joy deepens. You might even lose your car keys less often!

Where there is peace and meditation,
there is neither anxiety nor doubt.
—ST. FRANCIS OF ASSISI

When you take the time each day to sit quietly, with no other requirement than remaining alert and relaxed, you allow the stable, clear, confident person you truly are to emerge. The nagging voices that demanded attention, pushing you to do more, be different, all quiet down. In their place, there's a safe, open stillness. In that stillness you stand a good chance of discovering that:

- you're not responsible for everything,
- you can choose how you respond when your buttons get pushed,
- you're not alone or disconnected,
- impossible situations can be so absurd they're actually funny, and
- your world is a pretty amazing place.

Each of us falls victim to habits that take over and drive us places we'd rather not go. The good news is that you can learn to use the power of that habit-forming tendency to develop some worthwhile patterns for a change. Your regular meditation practice is a good place to start. The simple, non-judgmental view from your cushion can gently reveal some of the self-defeating habits you've fallen into and help you loosen their grip by adjusting your priorities.

Learning to meditate is like learning to read. It's a basic skill. Why you want to learn to read and what you choose to read are mostly up to you. Why you want to learn to meditate and how you bring meditation into the rest of your life is up to you as well.

WHAT SCIENCE SAYS
ABOUT MEDITATION

There's growing evidence that your brain can change and develop as long as you live. Meditation produces changes in the brain that can affect your body and even your emotions. This chapter is not a review of science articles complete with footnotes and references. It points to the main areas of study and some of the results. To follow up, if you're interested, use the Internet (Google "meditation and insomnia," for example) or ask your reference librarian for help finding studies.

That said, here's a brief overview. In the 1970s, a cardiologist named Herbert Benson, at Harvard Medical School, turned his research on very simple forms of meditation into a bestseller called *The Relaxation Response*. He confirmed that his patients could reduce their heart rates by meditating regularly. However, until the 1990s the technology didn't exist to measure changes in brain functioning and blood composition while someone was actually in a state of meditation.

Now scientists are discovering fascinating things about

how our brains work and how that affects our bodies and our emotions by studying the brains of meditators.

Hospitals across the country are offering meditation programs to their patients to help them deal with pain. At the University of Pittsburgh, for instance, a group of people 65 and older who suffered chronic lower back pain had "significantly greater pain acceptance and physical function" after just eight weeks of meditation training.

Similar results are reported in cases of fibromyalgia and rheumatoid arthritis, and meditation has proven useful in lessening the incidence and severity of asthma attacks.

One of the most interesting discoveries is that meditation actually enhances the effect of some standard medical treatments. For example:

- Several weeks after being given a flu shot, meditators tested higher in their ability to resist infection than a control group.
- Psoriasis sufferers found that they could make their ultraviolet light treatments four times more effective by meditating during the treatment.
- Meditation has been used to help alleviate insomnia and mild to moderate depression.

Regular meditation tends to produce lower heart rate, blood pressure, and respiration, and scientists believe that may explain its ability to reduce a person's level of anxiety. It also affects your general tendency to get angry. How does it do that?

The key here is brain plasticity. It means you can not

only change your mind, your experience actually changes your brain. Richard Davidson at the University of Wisconsin and Jon Kabat-Zin at the University of Massachusetts Medical School found that meditators typically have greater activity in the left frontal cortex, while anxious, stressed, or depressed people have an overactive right side. Meditators (and people who are typically calm and happy) recover faster from negative events and have higher levels of immune system function.

You don't have to meditate for years before you see results. University of Oregon students were trained in mindfulness meditation to see if it would help them focus their attention and filter out distractions. After just five days the meditators out-performed a group that did relaxation exercises on a test of attention. They were also better at handling stress. When given a difficult math quiz, the meditators had lower levels of the hormone cortisol in their saliva. The body produces cortisol under stress.

Of course, the more experience you accumulate as a meditator, the more the beneficial changes persist between meditation sessions. You don't just feel more compassion for a friend who's your focus during loving kindness meditation (discussed later in the book). Compassion becomes your response to suffering wherever you find it.

And here's some great news: Researchers at Emory University in Atlanta found that elderly regular Zen meditators didn't show the brain shrinkage and decline in attention of nonmeditators of the same age.

The most beautiful thing we can experience
is the mysterious. It is the source of
all true art and science.

—ALBERT EINSTEIN

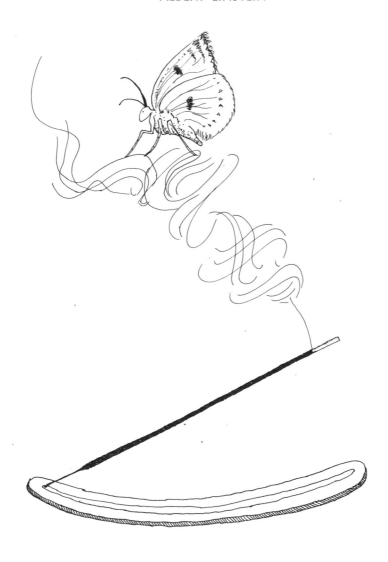

GETTING
STARTED

JUMP RIGHT IN—SIT RIGHT DOWN

It's about time to get a taste of what meditation is. Read through the following numbered steps and give it a try.

1. First, think about where you can be for about ten minutes without any disturbance. It's hard to find a really quiet place these days, but do the best you can. If you can't turn off the ringer on your phone, muffle it with a pillow. Tell whoever happens to be in the house that you need a short time alone. Close the door.

2. Sit comfortably. Cartoons always show a meditating figure sitting cross-legged on the ground, but you don't need to do that. Meditation can work just as well in a chair, although preferably not an armchair with soft cushions that swallow you whole when you relax. In fact, if this is your first try at meditation, use a chair. You'll find more suggestions for sitting alternatives in later chapters.

3. Sit in an upright but relaxed position. You don't need to be ramrod straight—your back has a natural curve to it. However, it's better not to lean against the back of your chair if you're sitting in one.

4. Rest your hands in your lap or on your thighs.

5. Close your eyes, especially if this is your first try, so there will be less distraction.

6. Take three deep breaths and release any tension you notice in your body.

7. Sit still, as relaxed as you can be, just being aware of your breathing. Without changing your breathing pattern in any way, just count ten breaths.

When you've done that, open your eyes and notice if anything feels different from the way it did when you first sat down.

If something does feel different, just notice what it is. No two meditation sessions are exactly alike, so whatever you experienced this time may or may not happen again. That's why it's good to begin each session with a sense of freshness. If you're always a beginner, you're always open to discoveries.

If nothing seems different, that's fine too. Maybe you're a natural and this was just the first tiny step of the adventure. Or it could be that you've just discovered one reason why it's called meditation *practice*. It's easy to describe the outside, but the inside process takes time to accomplish.

If you find yourself distracted, bored, or frustrated, think of that attitude as your "two-year-old" mind. It knows there's something there and it wants it—but it wants it now, so it's whining and banging its spoon on the table. A wise parent gently helps the kid see that's not the way to get what it wants.

GETTING BETTER AT IT

There are many ways to make entering into meditation easier. The outside ones are simpler to describe, so let's start there.

Wear comfortable, loose clothing. If you're going to sit on the floor, you'll soon get to know which of your pants are still comfortable after you've been sitting for a while, and which ones bind or cut off your circulation so your foot or your rear end falls asleep!

Keep a shawl or a small blanket within arm's reach to put over your knees or around your shoulders if you feel chilly.

Choose a position to hold your hands. Some people like to sit "pretending to be a Buddha." In this position, you place your right hand crosswise in your lap, palm up. Then place your left hand on top, palm up, so the tips of your thumbs can touch. Or you may prefer to sit with your hands resting palm downward on your thighs.

Try to keep your hands still until you take a break. You can experiment with another position in your next session, if you like. This is the beginning of asking your body to put up with being ignored for a short time because you have something to do with your mind. The idea is to make that body as comfy as possible, so it can just quiet down for a bit.

You can begin with your eyes closed to help you calm down. After a few minutes, open them, leaving them half-closed, with your gaze soft, aimed at about a 45-degree angle downward. You're not looking at anything in particular, but you're not shutting out the world, either. Meditating with eyes open serves several purposes: First, you're less likely to fall asleep. If you feel yourself getting drowsy or drifty, just raise your eyes. That often perks up the mind. If you're in an agitated state, with thoughts whirling through your brain, lower your gaze slightly and take a few deep breaths. Finally, meditating with your eyes open underlines the fact that you're not trying to escape the world (a strategy that rarely works anyway), but learning to live with things as they are.

If you need to blink, go ahead. If you need to swallow, do it. But try to keep scratching, fidgeting, and shifting around to a minimum. If something itches, just notice it and be grateful. It'll keep you from falling asleep. It's a sign you're still alive.

Your sitting posture is important enough that we'll give it the whole next section.

Skill to do comes of doing.
—RALPH WALDO EMERSON

GET A GOOD SEAT

If I say "imagine a meditator," chances are your picture involves a person sitting cross-legged on the ground. In many parts of the world, that's the way meditation is taught. There are good reasons for this tradition.

Sitting on the ground is a way of grounding yourself. It can remind you that you're not trying to escape into your imagination.

So of course you can sit on the ground (or, more likely, on the floor), but you can also meditate sitting in a chair, lying on the couch, jogging on the track, or perched on the edge of a hospital bed, holding somebody's hand. As long as you've got your mind with you, you can meditate.

Nonetheless, having a position you usually take to meditate in can be a powerful reminder of what you want to do. Sitting upright with your back straight—not stiff or strained—is helpful. Imagine your spine like a stack of golden coins. That position, with your hands at rest, helps to initiate a state of calm clarity. Why not give yourself the best support you can for this adventure?

Most Westerners find the full lotus position, legs crossed and feet resting on the opposite thighs, just too uncomfortable. If you can do it, bravo! But the point is to sit so you're stable and comfortable enough to be there a while. If you want to sit on the floor, try pulling one foot up in front to rest against your bottom and put the other one in front of that.

You can also sit cross-legged, with your ankles crossed. Tuck a small pillow or a rolled-up towel under each knee for support. A soft rug will ease the pressure on your ankles.

And remember, it's fine to sit on a chair as long as your feet are flat on the floor. It's best if you don't lean against the chair back, but you can if necessary.

The important thing is to find a position where your body isn't complaining and distracting you from the work you need to do with your mind.

Those who wish to sing, always find a song.
—SWEDISH PROVERB

YOUR OWN MOUNTAINTOP

Packing a few necessities and heading for a mountaintop is entirely optional to establishing a firm meditation practice. But it is a good idea to give some thought to creating the environment you'll be spending some time in.

Quiet: Find the balance that works for you. Too much sound is a distraction—you'll spend more energy ignoring it. But some people find that total absence of sound leads to napping. Not that naps are a bad thing, but that's not what you sat down to do. To limit noise pollution, if you've closed any relevant doors, you might consider ear plugs, moving to a different room, or even playing very soft music through headphones if nothing else seems to be working. Soft music can help when it's too quiet as well.

Temperature: Do you need a small portable heater? Or a fan? Having a hot beverage or some ice water available during breaks can help your body adjust if adjusting your environment isn't a possibility.

Light level: You don't want it too bright or too dark for starters. Experiment with a lamp you can move around.

Fresh air: Although you don't want it drafty, a good sup-ply of oxygen helps keep you alert. A stuffy room feels heavy and uninspiring.

Your visual background: When you do open your eyes in your meditation, think about what you'll see. A window view can be uplifting or distracting. Facing a messy room or a desk full of reminders of work can steal your attention.

Many traditions suggest sitting in front of a small table that you use only for your meditation practice. It serves as a visual focus, a point that you can bring your mind back to. You can put a candle, flower or small plant, framed picture of something meaningful to you, or a crystal on it. Make it attractive. If you like, you can burn incense to clear the air of household odors.

When you sit down in the space you've created, the habit you've built up of relaxing and entering into meditation will make each session easier to begin.

And whenever you pass by your special place during the day, let the sense of meditative calm return to you like the remembered sound of a bell.

You cannot teach a man anything;
you can only help him to find it for himself.
—GALILEO GALILEI

BRING YOUR BODY ALONG

Perhaps you're interested in learning how to meditate because you feel tense and stressed out far too much of the time. In that case, being told to relax before you can meditate seems pretty dumb. Your body doesn't rack up that tension on its own. It's your mind that turns the screws, and meditation will calm your mind.

The fact is, relaxing the body is the first step in meditation, and it's worth learning how to do. You can practice relaxation at the end of your day, when it's hard to let go of the things that have happened and hard to stop thinking about tomorrow. A relaxation session can make falling asleep easier and improve the quality of the sleep you get. You can also do a short version during the day when you feel the tension beginning to build up.

Meditation is not about some state;
it is about the meditator.
—CHARLOTTE JOKO BECK

The first time you do this exercise, sit in a chair with your feet on the floor and your arms relaxed and hanging at your sides. If your chair has arms, you can rest your arms on them, but let your hands dangle if you can.

1. **Close your eyes.**

2. **Bring your attention to your feet** and ankles. Feel any tension in them loosening and relaxing. It may help to imagine that you're sitting with your feet in a gently flowing stream. The water is just the temperature you'd like it to be. Any tension or tiredness in your feet and ankles is carried away by the stream.

3. **Move your attention up to your calves.** Relax any tension in your lower legs. You can picture the tension flowing down to your feet and being carried away by the stream.

4. **Continue moving your attention** up to your thighs, then your abdomen, back, and chest, loosening and relaxing each area in its turn and letting the tension flow away.

5. **Tell your body what to do.** Use words like releasing, relaxing, sinking, smoothing, opening.

6. **After you've relaxed your chest,** relax your hands, arms, shoulders, neck, and face.

Then just take a moment to notice your breathing. It should be deep and slow.

Now as you breathe out, say the word "one" to yourself, silently. As you breathe in, say "one." Keep saying "one" over and over, until the end of your session. Aim for 15 or 20 minutes total the first time. Don't use a timer for this exercise. You can put a clock within sight and open your eyes from time to time if you want to.

After you've done this exercise sitting up, you can try it lying down. If you do it in bed when you're ready to fall asleep you may find yourself drifting off into a deep sleep—which is not a bad thing!

A LITTLE MIND MUSIC

You've got your cushion plumped up and your candle lit. You're suited up and ready to meditate. You tell yourself, "release and relax." Your body feels like warm clouds.

This must be what it's all about.

Well, you're close. Now that you've got the outside pretty well organized, the real stuff can begin.

Turn your mind inward. What does that mean? Well, you can use the image of your hands facing outward, held up in front of your face. Imagine that you simply turn them inward, so your palms face in. Usually your mind is turned outward: you're looking at things, planning where you're going, watching out for things to avoid, thinking about what to do next instead of what you're doing in the moment.

But now you're sitting in a safe, well-prepared place. There's nothing out there you haven't seen already. With no agenda and no expectations, just turn your attention around, inward. And sit there.

Pretty soon your mind starts up. Your leg itches. Did you

turn off the phone? There's a funny thumping noise—hope it's not the washer. Thoughts keep rattling through.

Here's where meditation methods can really help. There are many, from different traditions. You already know the basic one. Watch your breath. Whenever your mind wanders, bring it gently back, like a puppy on a leash. Watch your breath. Don't get angry or annoyed. Thinking is what your mind has been trained to do. That's its job. Now you're going to learn to keep your attention focused on something even if the mind wants to check your calendar or see if the dog needs water.

The composer Stravinsky had written a new piece with a difficult violin passage. After rehearsing for several weeks, the solo violinist came to the composer and said he was sorry, but the passage was too difficult. No violinist could play it. Stravinsky said, "I understand that. What I am after is the sound of someone trying to play it."

—THOMAS POWERS

FREE THE MENTAL FIVE

At the start of meditation practice there are five common roadblocks that people set up for themselves. You can think of them as five attitude problems, five excuses, or five game plans for failure.

1. I can't do this.

You *can* do this. Just think—thousands of people all over the world, from Iceland to Patagonia, are doing it right now. And the only goal is doing it. The only way you can fail is to not do it.

2. I should be doing something.

You already are. When you're meditating, you're doing something that improves everything else you do. A calmer, clearer mind will help you be more efficient, and you'll see more clearly what you should be doing.

3. I can't stop my thoughts.

Guess what? You're normal! Meditation isn't about stopping your thoughts. It's about changing your attitude toward thoughts. They come; they go. Learn a simple exercise in focusing attention, like watching your breath, and you'll be on the way to seeing those thoughts like a wise old grandparent, watching the children play.

4. I'm afraid of what I'll see.

There's nothing inside there that you don't already know. In fact, you'll find out you can be stronger and more stable than you ever imagined, and you'll develop tools to deal with sorrow, pain, and fear.

5. I'll probably get bored.

Boredom means that you gave up. Living with attention is the opposite of boredom! Meditation develops your ability to be more aware and more alive. It's not about sitting there, spaced out, totally blank. It's about expanding your capacity to see, feel, and respond in the very moment.

Accept what you can't change, change what you can, and hold any commitment to growth and betterment lightly in your hands. That doesn't mean you're not serious. It's the difference between grasping onto that desire to grow or setting it down to watch where it wants to go and being ready to help it get there or guide it away from an edge.

In meditation we are continuously discovering who and what we are.

—SAKYONG MIPHAM RINPOCHE

YOUR
MEDITATION
TOOLBOX

MOTIVATION

Your meditation toolbox contains a number of resources and options to help you establish your practice in the beginning, and to refresh it as you go along. Motivation is the most important item you can put in that toolbox. Without a clear sense of why you're interested in meditation, it's unlikely that you'll stay with it long enough to get any of its benefits.

Why do you want to learn to meditate? Health reasons? Curiosity? Part of a spiritual path? This is your own business, but take some time to think about it. Maybe reading this book has given you some additional reasons. It's a good idea to write down what interests you and what you hope to get out of sitting practice. If you find yourself going a few days without sitting, reread what you wrote. You can reinspire yourself better than anyone else because you know what your issues and interests are.

Check in with yourself regularly. Remember that the point isn't to sit in a particular position every time or to practice longer and longer. The method isn't the meditation.

Meditation is the place you get to—the calm, clear, totally alive person you are right then, in the moment.

Think about it. Do you find yourself feeling less tense? Have you noticed a difference in how you meet frustration after you've meditated? Maybe you feel a little less swallowed up by other people's demands on you. Maybe you've noticed how other people react when they're caught up and miserable and how that spreads around them.

When your buttons get pushed, what do you do? What do other people do that gets to you? When you see one of those button-pushers coming at you, can you take a deep breath and remember the calm, clear place you got to on your cushion? Sometime you'll just let the problem pass on by like water passing over stones. What other people do is their business. Your business has to do with maintaining your balance in a rocky world.

Meditation is about living a full, sane, happy life.

A man of meditation is happy,
not for an hour or a day,
but quite round the circle of all his years.
—ISAAC TAYLOR

MINDFULNESS

Mindfulness is one of those words that people suddenly seem to be using in everyday life. If I were just more mindful, I wouldn't always forget where I put things down. Have you ever thought that? It's true that mindfulness as we're going to use the word has to do with attention, and that distraction is the opposite of mindfulness.

But the most interesting thing about mindfulness is that it naturally expands as you practice it. The simple exercise suggested earlier in which you become aware of your breath is a good basic mindfulness practice. If you spend ten minutes every day sitting quietly and focusing on your breath, you might be surprised to find yourself naturally paying attention to other things in the course of your day—how you hand a book to someone, how you stand in an elevator, how you leave the things on your desk at the end of the day.

Meditation is basically a way of being fully present in the moment, and mindfulness is a way to get there from a scattered state.

Here's an example: You're reading this sentence. Are you aware of your eyes tracking along the line of words? Are you sounding the words in your mind? Can you expand that awareness to include the rest of your body? Are you sitting down? Can you notice the feeling of the chair seat? Are you standing in the aisle of the bookstore? What can you smell in the air wherever you are?

You may find it easier to remain aware of yourself when you're moving. But if you decide to put this book down and go off to do something, how long can you remember to keep that extra flavor of mindfulness, of being aware that you're doing something?

It's said that an old woman once approached the Buddha and asked him how she could learn to meditate. He told her to be aware of her hands as she drew water from the well. He knew that paying attention to her hands would help her stop the chatter in her mind and give her a taste of a calm state. Once she had that experience, she could find that calmness by paying attention in other simple movements. And soon she might find that state of calm arising when she simply sat in her chair at home. And she'd be meditating.

Mindfulness is the door to freedom.
—B. ALAN WALLACE

USING AN OBJECT

If your meditation space includes a table, you may already have set some objects on it that you find meaningful—photos or pictures, statues, crystals, flowers, or candles. Your arrangement can be as simple or as full as you like. It's meant to inspire you, so it's entirely up to you.

Experiment. A photograph of someone in your life may draw you to sit down, but you may find yourself distracted by your own stories about that person. In that case, something pleasing but more neutral might be a better choice. The idea is to give your eyes something to rest on. A small votive candle or a single flower works well.

Sit comfortably in front of your chosen object. Take three deep breaths to settle down.

Sit so your gaze can rest downward. If you've chosen a candle, note that you're not staring into the light or trying to shut out everything else. You're just letting your gaze rest lightly on the flame. Try to remain mindful of your body and your surroundings.

When you notice your mind wandering, just turn your attention back to your object and let go of your other thoughts. You're training your mind to stay still. There's nothing to do but notice whether your body is relaxed and your attention is where you meant to leave it.

Give yourself a time limit. Start with five minutes. Then stand up and stretch and go back to sitting if you like.

You can do the same exercise with an object or an image you imagine or visualize. Some people have a favorite sacred picture or statue that's so familiar it's easy to recall. Hold that image in your mind. This is training your mind to focus on something without allowing yourself to get distracted.

When you find your mind wandering, and realize that you've forgotten about the picture in your head, don't get annoyed or cross with yourself. Just bring the image back.

If you don't feel you can imagine a picture clearly enough, consider that what's important isn't the actual image, but what you feel about it. If you're a Christian, you might remember a particular picture of Christ that shows great strength or caring. Hold that feeling as your focus while you sit just remembering the picture. The point is to give your mind something to do that keeps it, and you, present without wandering off into plans for the future or memories of the past.

Remember: a method is only a means, not the meditation itself. It is through practicing the method skillfully that you reach the perfection of that pure state of total presence which is the real meditation.
—SOGYAL RINPOCHE

MIND YOUR MANTRA

A mantra is a phrase that's repeated, either aloud or in your mind, as part of a practice. In some traditions, mantras are said to be words that protect the mind. In our case, they protect the mind from wandering off in all directions.

Chanting a mantra just means repeating it, over and over. Sometimes there's a melody associated with the mantra so that it's almost like singing it, but it can also just be spoken words. As you repeat your mantra, pay attention to your own voice, to the sound you're making.

Some spiritual teachers give their students personal mantras. But there are mantras that have been used for centuries in different traditions and you're free to choose one of those. You can find a collection of them on pages 85 and 86.

You've probably seen the Sanskrit syllable "OM" (see page 58) perhaps as a design or a car decal. You say it as you breathe out—ooooohmmmm—lengthening the sound. Begin the sound in the back of your mouth and gradually move it toward the front until your lips close at the "mmm." Then you breathe in and start again.

Okay. I know. This is what they always use in sitcoms when they want a character to be really weird. She sits cross-legged on the floor with her eyes shut, chanting "om" and ignoring everybody. But the fact is that in the Hindu tradition, this is one of the most powerful mantras. It doesn't really have a meaning, but it's been described as the sound that has been here since the creation of the universe. It's considered a holy sound that leads toward enlightenment. Try it sometime when nobody's around and you're going to start your meditation session. Just say the word three times and then sit. See if you feel different after you've chanted.

Mantras are especially useful when you're emotionally worked up over something, when it's your time to sit, but you're distracted by worry, anger, or fear. Try this:

1. **Go to your meditation place** and get ready to sit.

2. **Remind yourself why you're meditating** and what your intention is for this session ("I'm going to sit for 20 minutes, in 5-minute sessions, with stretch breaks in between.")

3. **Check your posture** and decide whether you want to start with your eyes closed or half-open.

4. **Notice the feelings in your body.** Is your throat tight? Does your face feel warm?

5. **Choose a mantra** and begin repeating it, aloud if possible. Keep this up for the first five minutes. Just work on being aware of the sound you're making without judging it or changing it too much.

6. At the end of 5 minutes, check to see if the feelings are still the same in your body.

7. Repeat as often as you need to.

It's possible that after a while you might discover that you're thinking about something else or daydreaming while the chant goes on! This is not a recommended form of multitasking. Bring your mind back to the sound of the chant.

As you get used to chanting, you can use the mantra practice whenever something happens that's upsetting, like being stuck in traffic—road rage is hard on the mind and body. Try chanting a loud mantra for a minute. Standing in lines can be frustrating. You can let a mantra run through your head and do a little mind training instead of fidgeting. And so on.

*Meditation is not to escape from society, but to come
back to ourselves and see what is going on.
Once there is seeing, there must be acting.
With mindfulness, we know what to do
and what not to do to help.*
—THICH NHAT HANH

JUST PRACTICE—
YOU'RE ALREADY PERFECT

PUT DOWN THAT PIANO

Most people who meditate talk about having a "practice." Usually that means they do something daily, or at least regularly, involving some or all of the techniques described in the earlier chapters. If you really want to enjoy the benefits of meditation, it's time to think about establishing your own practice.

For many people, "practice" was something your Mom made you do, sitting on a piano bench when you really wanted to be outside. This is different. Your meditation practice will help you deal with the places in your life that are difficult, unclear, and unsatisfactory.

But like many endeavors, you'll get the most out of your effort if you do it regularly. It's better to sit for a short time every day, at the same time, than to say "I'll do it on the weekend when I have time." The weekend warrior approach doesn't work for dieting or learning the violin or for developing a solid meditation practice.

So start with ten minutes a day for the first week. Don't

expect to achieve transcendent bliss by day three, but don't beat yourself up over it, either. It not only gets easier to settle your mind as the days pass, you'll probably find yourself looking forward to your private time.

Don't think of your practice as a chore. If you find yourself getting bored or antsy, try a different technique. If you've been just watching your breath, try using an object. Try out a mantra. Re-read what you wrote about why you want to do this. Start bringing your meditation into your ordinary life. (See "Quick Fixes for Busy Folks".) But come back to basic sitting at least once a week.

> *Knowing is not enough; we must apply.*
> *Willing is not enough; we must do.*
> —JOHANN WOLFGANG VON GOETHE

BOOK YOUR TIME

Feeling that there's never enough time to do everything we have to do is one of the main sources of stress in our lives. So we're supposed to deal with this stress about limited time by adding another "have-to" in the form of sitting meditation every single day?

Yes, and here's how that works. We waste a tremendous amount of time and energy in worry, inefficient action, indecision, negativity, and confusion. Mindfulness practice spreads over from simple awareness of the body in motion to greater care in actions and greater access to memory. Similarly, establishing a reliable connection to a state of emotional balance, mental calm, and clarity helps sort out our priorities and simply do what needs doing without the drama and distraction of the soap opera we're tempted to create. If you don't waste your energy in fear of what might happen next or anxiety over what might not, you'll be able to deal with what does happen (and maybe enjoy it) a whole lot more.

Daily sittings should become a habit. We all know how

easy it is to acquire bad habits. Well, guess what. Good habits aren't that hard to take up, too. You make appointments for important things in your life. This is an important thing. Plan those daily sessions into your schedule. Use a timer if you need to, or just put a clock where you can easily check the time.

But don't short-change yourself. A short nap can give you a boost in the afternoon, but you need a full night's sleep, too. Give yourself a chance to really learn the art of meditation by keeping your daily commitment, however short it may have to be. Then on the weekend, give yourself permission to go deeper by spending a good half hour or more.

If you can, meditate in the morning before you get caught up in your day. Spending time in a state of focused, relaxed equilibrium makes coping with stressful situations easier later in the day. If you're just not a morning person and it's all you can do to get out of the house in the morning, try the evening—but before you get sleepy. Resist the urge to replay your day during your sitting session, especially if you tend to go off onto "I should have told him. . . ." That's a surefire way to waste your time. Let your session be both the end of your day and the beginning of the next—a time that is uncluttered and ready for possibilities.

Some people think that meditation takes time away from physical accomplishment. Taken to extremes, of course, that's true. Most people, however, find that meditation creates more time than it takes.
—PETER McWILLIAMS

WRITE YOURSELF UP

Many people enjoy keeping a record of their meditation adventure. If you're willing do it, make it a serious effort. Buy a notebook that's just for this purpose. Begin by recording your motives for starting on this journey.

Traditionally, this journal is called your Book of Insights. You'll find it useful after the first flush of enthusiasm calms down and you start wondering if you're really doing anything by just sitting there. Let your notebook remind you why you're taking this path and what you've already found on the way. Rereading your original intention every once in a while can reinspire you. Record how your life seems to be changing as a result of your practice.

It's a good idea to record your practice plan, too. Check it weekly and see what's working and what isn't. Change what doesn't work. If mornings are just too hectic, try evenings. If the floor is too hard or too drafty, try sitting on the couch or your bed. Keep alert for other times during the day when you might insert a brief session of meditation and jot them down for future reference.

Set aside a few minutes weekly to write in your book. Of course, if you're used to journaling, you might want to do it daily. Record things that seem different: you noticed how a co-worker always gets angry at something, but doesn't do anything to change the situation—just complains. This time, you didn't get caught up in the drama. Somebody did something stupid on the road and you just shook your head at how crazy some people can be.

Keep your Book of Insights and a pen wherever you meditate at home. It's an official part of your meditation toolkit. Just noticing it there might spark a memory of something you wanted to write down and you can do it right then.

We either make ourselves miserable,
or we make ourselves strong.
The amount of work is the same.
—CARLOS CASTANEDA

QUICK FIXES
FOR BUSY FOLKS

ACTIVE MEDITATION

Once you've learned what meditation is in a quiet, undemanding setting, you can enter that state while you're on the go. That's good news, because people usually spend a lot more time moving from place to place than sitting quietly in a quiet room. Trying to learn meditation from scratch while running for a bus is like taking swimming lessons in a rough ocean. It's much better to get your feet wet in the pool first. But you can use simple movement early on.

Try walking meditation:

1. Sit for five minutes.

2. Keep your mindfulness and alertness while you stand up and walk around the room three times. You're in a room you know, so there shouldn't be too much distraction. Walk slowly. Pay attention to your body.

3. Sit down again and meditate for five minutes.

4. Stand up and take a moment to feel your weight on the soles of your feet.

5. Now walk slowly around the room again. This time,

notice and say (in your head, if you want) "lifting, pushing," as you go forward, "dropping" as your foot touches the ground again. This should take quite a while to do. If you find yourself thinking about something else, stop where you are and say "thinking." Then go back to focusing on your walking.

Experiment with different amounts of time in sitting and walking. Experienced meditators who do walking meditation may alternate sitting for 20 minutes or half an hour with walking slowly for five minutes.

Once you've got the idea, try walking mindfully on some route that's familiar to you. Do it for five minutes on the way to the bus stop or on the way home. Try to be mindful of your body moving without thinking about anything else. If you get distracted, just say "thinking" and go back to paying attention to your body, walking. If you're afraid people will think you're weird walking slowly, go to a botanical garden where you could be looking at plants or a museum where you could be looking at pictures or stuffed animals.

After a few days of practice, you'll find that you can walk slowly, but not so slowly that you seem odd. You'll just look as if you're thinking about something.

Life shrinks or expands
according to one's courage.
—ANAÏS NIN

ANY TIME, ANY PLACE . . .

As meditation becomes less something you do and more a part of the way you are, allow that mindful way of doing things to expand into more of your daily life. Remember the old woman whom the Buddha told to be aware of her hands when drawing water from the well? For us, too, water is a precious commodity and it's getting scarce. Take a moment before you turn on the faucet to appreciate the ease with which we get pure water. Do you know where yours comes from? Be grateful for it and mindful as you turn it on. May all beings have such pure water.

When you eat your next meal, slow down a little. Really taste the food in your next bite. How many people did it take to get that food onto your plate? Eat mindfully for a while, with a sense of appreciation for all their efforts. May all beings have nourishment.

Working at the computer, try not to get lost in the screen and the keyboard. Take a few minutes just to sit there with your hands in your lap, eyes closed, and focus on your breath.

Count ten breaths and open your eyes. If anybody asks, tell them you're helping your head work better.

When you're stuck in traffic, crawling along at an idling pace, remember your walking meditation. Or just recall the calm of your last sitting meditation. Think about the fact that all around you are fragile human bodies in plastic and metal boxes. Drive mindfully, with a sense of caring for those other bodies. It's so much better for you than pounding the steering wheel in frustration or bellowing at the traffic jam ahead of you. Stress hormones are hard on bodies.

Some people find public transportation a great place to meditate. Practice with your eyes lowered and you'll look like most of the people around you. Hey—how many of them do you think might be meditating?

The more you bring meditation into your daily life, the healthier your life becomes. Does this mean you never get angry again? Well, meditation isn't a shortcut to sainthood. But you'll probably find that it's easier to stop yourself from flying off the handle. And all you need is a moment to consider if whatever situation got you steamed would really be eased by your anger. You can still use your "I'm Serious About This" voice when it's needed. But you'll be in charge. And you might find yourself feeling sorry for the poor guys who need to waste their energy grousing and antagonizing other people.

The most instructive experiences are those of everyday life.
—FRIEDRICH NIETZSCHE

ADVANCED
STUFF

REACHING OUT

Yes, meditating regularly will change you. But it won't make something grow that wasn't already there and ready to sprout. Here's something to think about: The mind isn't the only muscle group that gets exercised in meditation practice. The heart develops, too. What begins to shrink is the selfish, demanding, touchy, impossible-to-satisfy bully or diva that lives inside each of us and makes life miserable for everybody.

You may find yourself feeling deeply sorry for people who are suffering the frustrations and disappointments of life but have no resources to deal with their reactions. Loving kindness or compassion practices give you a way to spread the good stuff you're generating. They're a form of directed meditation, or contemplation, that's a little different from simple sitting. Here's a starter.

1. Sit for five minutes.

2. Remember a time when you were truly loved—when you felt respected, cherished, protected, and secure in the experience of that love.

3. Let the warmth of that feeling fill your heart. Sit with that feeling for a few minutes.

4. Return that love. Whoever it was who loved you, remember them. Let that love and gratitude for that love fill your heart. Return that love. Wherever they may be, they're alive and present now in your memory.

5. Return to the wellspring of feeling in your heart and sit with it.

6. Now let that feeling flow out into the world wherever it can go. Think about people and places where it might be in short supply. You'll find that personal feeling of love changing into compassion for all the beings who are alone, in danger, and fearful.

7. Return to simple sitting for a few minutes before you end the session.

The more you do this kind of practice, the more you'll find your negative reactions turning into responses of understanding and compassion. You'll take things less personally, and you'll avoid confrontations as much for the good of the other guy as for your own peace of mind.

Peace of mind is one of the benefits of meditation. Enjoy it and spread it around!

We cannot live only for ourselves. A thousand fibers connect us with our fellow men; and among those fibers, as sympathetic threads, our actions run as causes, and they come back to us as effects.
—HERMAN MELVILLE

GROUPS AND CLASSES

B eing with a group of people who are all doing the same thing can be useful. Sitting with people who are comfortable just being quiet together is pretty unusual. And those same quiet people are often glad to talk (afterwards) about how meditation fits into their lives, how they cope with challenges, and what they do as "practice."

You'll find those groups in community colleges, adult schools, hospitals, clinics, churches, and senior centers. Many classes are specifically geared toward stress relief; others may be part of a religious practice.

Check out bulletin boards in coffee houses and health food stores. Inquire at a local hospital or clinic. Wherever there are classes offered for adults, there might be a class in meditation. In larger cities, there may be a "Meditation Instruction" section in the yellow pages of the phone book. Or you can Google "Meditation Instruction" and the name of your hometown, just to see what comes up. Craig's List, if it's available in your area, may overwhelm you with opportunities.

You might want to experience different approaches to meditation, from the ritual and formality of Zen Buddhism to the fellowship of a circle of chairs in the community center.

If you decide to check out one of these offerings, it's a good idea to call ahead and ask if they sit on the floor and if you need to bring your own cushion. Is a fee or donation expected? Is the meditation offered as part of a particular spiritual tradition? If the notice you found doesn't say, you might want to ask who's leading, or teaching, the session. For a beginner, the best introduction can come from a person whose only qualification is being a regular meditator who has found it to be of real value in life.

Finally, don't be surprised if you're asked to remove your shoes before entering the meditation room. It's a sign of respect in some traditions and a symbol that you're willing to leave your connection to the dust and problems of the road outside.

It is one of the most beautiful compensations of this life that no man can sincerely try to help another without helping himself.
—RALPH WALDO EMERSON

FINDING A TEACHER

When some meditators use the word "teacher," they're referring to a spiritual guide.

If you want to explore meditation as part of a spiritual practice, you might want to find a Japanese roshi, Indian swami, Tibetan lama, Christian teacher of Centering Prayer, or another respected instructor who brings not only deep personal experience, but also the wisdom of a long tradition to the responsibility of introducing beginners to meditation.

How do you find the one that's right for you? There's an old Hindu saying, "When the student is ready, the teacher appears." But that's not usually the way we do things. Go to the library or bookstore and spend a little time browsing through books on meditation. Get a sense of how different teachers and traditions talk about meditation. What's the goal? What are the benefits? If they use the word "enlightenment," how is it described?

When you find something that appeals, see if the book lists centers with classes. If not, write down the name of the kind of meditation and/or the main authority who's mentioned. The previous section addressed ways to find ongoing meditation groups and classes. Check those resources for connections to the person or type of meditation you fancy.

Use your common sense and intuition (which the meditation practice you may have already started helps you develop). Go with what "feels right." Steer clear of groups or so-called teachers who make you feel uncomfortable, who charge huge fees, or who pressure you to sign up for more than you want to on your first visit.

Nonetheless, do recognize that making a connection to a spiritual teacher is a serious step. Although all responsible teachers expect people to try out a variety of approaches and experience a number of teachers before making a commitment to a particular path, most traditions say that when you ask a teacher to take you on as a student, you're making a connection that will affect the teacher as well as affecting you. This isn't a bad thing. It means that when you say "I'll sit in meditation for 20 minutes every day," you're making that promise to yourself, and you're also involving another person—your teacher.

If you let yourself get distracted by work, or friends, or other interests, and you don't fulfill that promise, it not only diminishes you, but it weakens your connection to your spiritual path and to your teacher as well. Just knowing that helps some practitioners stay the course.

It's a good idea to be clear about why you're interested in meditation in general and why you feel drawn to a particular type of meditation or teacher. That's something you can "sit with." Just lightly hold the recognition that you're interested in Insight Meditation, or drawn to what you know about Thich Nhat Hahn, for example, and see where your mind takes you. Being clear about your motivation lets a teacher know how to help.

Since it's easier to be centered and quiet away from the

demands of your ordinary life, many meditators enjoy going on retreat, often in beautiful natural settings. To jumpstart a practice or refresh one that's running out of steam, consider going on retreat with a group or a teacher you find interesting.

The best teacher is the one who suggests rather than dogmatizes, and inspires his listener with the wish to teach himself.

—EDWARD BULWER-LYTTON

MANY MANTRAS

This section describes the practice of chanting mantra in some detail because it's probably the meditation support method that's least familiar to us Westerners, and it's such a good resource to have.

A mantra isn't a phrase or sentence in the way we think of them. Many mantras can't be translated because the sounds in them aren't really words in any language. Instead, they're a kind of seed that can grow into the fulfillment of a wish or an intention. Chanting a mantra can help create a feeling or a state of mind. There are a number of explanations for why they work: The sounds themselves may have a particular power or effect—their vibrations are said to be aligned with basic human capacities. Or we may be hard-wired to respond to a repeated phrase by dropping our guard and our thoughts and entering a meditative state.

You use a mantra by sitting, relaxing, and repeating the phrase. You can repeat it aloud in a normal voice, or just in your head. Begin at the pace of regular talking and let the mantra lead you. Often as you become familiar with the mantra you'll find yourself speeding up. That's fine. Just go with the flow. Once you're used to the sound, use it to keep your mind present. Listen to the words as you say them. You may be surprised to discover, after a time, that you're actually reciting the mantra and thinking about something else! Just let that thought go and bring your mind back to the sound.

Here's a list of mantras to experiment with.

Om Mani Padme Hum
Buddhist—Sanskrit mantra of the Buddha of compassion

Om tare tu tare ture svaha
Buddhist—This mantra expresses the compassionate energy of Tara, the bodhisattva of compasion in female form. She is always ready to help beings in need.

Om bekanze, bekanze, maha bekanze, radzaya samudgate soha
The mantra which calls upon Medicine Buddha to eliminate the pain of illness whether physical, psychic, or the disruptive pain of a society gone wrong.

La ila'ha il'alahu
Islam—Arabic mantra proclaiming that God alone is worthy of worship.

Om Namah Shivaya
Hindu—This mantra means, "Salutations to that which I am capable of becoming." Its intention is to start one on the path of spiritual development.

Hare Krishna, Hare Krishna, Krishna Krishna, Hare Hare. Hare Rama, Hare Rama, Rama Rama, Hare Hare
(Pronounced Hah-ray) Hindu—expresses divine energy and joy.

Sabbe satt sukhi hontu
A Pali phrase meaning "May all beings be well (or happy)". Pali was the language the Buddha spoke.

Khamemi Savve Jiva, Savve Jiva Khamantu Me
Jain (an Indian religion characterized by universal nonvio-
lence)—"I grant forgiveness to all living beings. May all living
beings grant me forgiveness."

Om, shanti, shanti, shanti
Combines the primal word with your wish to bring about
peace in the universe

Shema Is'ra'el Adonai Eloheinu Adonai echad.
Jewish—"Hear, Oh Israel, the Lord our God, the Lord is One."

Namu amida butsu
Japanese Buddhist mantra for taking refuge in the Buddha of
Infinite Light.

Lord Jesus Christ, Son of God, have mercy on me.
Christian—from the Desert Fathers tradition.

Veni Sancte Spiritus
Christian—"Come Holy Spirit."

Earth I am, Fire I am, Water, Air, and Spirit I am
Pagan affirmation.

Isis, Astarte, Diana, Hecate, Demeter, Kali, Inanna
The names of the Goddess in the pagan tradition.

Single words can be chanted as mantras, too. Choose a
word that has significance for you—**shalom** or **shanti** (peace),
karuna (compassion), or **maranatha** (come, Lord). One way
to use a single word mantra is to take a full breath and then
say the word, prolonging the sound a bit if you wish. Let the
sound and the meaning the word holds for you resonate while

you finish the out breath and as you take your next breath. Say the word as you begin breathing out. Continue this pattern.

If you're familiar with a particular prayer from your own tradition, you might try reciting it while in a meditative state. Most traditional prayers can have a profound effect when given that kind of support. **Hail, Mary** is an obvious choice if you have a Catholic background. For Jews, **"Shema Israel,"** or just the first line of the prayer repeated, is effective. In fact, consider using just one line or so from any prayer that speaks to you: **"Lord, make me an instrument of thy peace,"** or St. Patrick's eloquent **"Christ with me, Christ before me, Christ behind me, Christ in me,"** or any lines from the Twenty-Third Psalm.

You can buy recorded chants to sing along with or to learn how to do some of the longer chants. Often the recordings have the words of the chants in the liner notes. The Internet has a number of sites with chants. Check out YouTube.com to hear some of the melodies used for chanting or to hear how the unfamiliar words are pronounced.

You may also create a personal matra in the form of an affirmation which, repeated in the calm, clear state of meditation increases its effectivness. Identify an area of your life that is important to you. Create a simple, positive statement that captures your intention or reflects the attitude you wish to express. Use words that engage your emotions.

**This day is full of opportunities for growth and joy.
I embrace them.**

I am doing the best I can, and so is everyone else

**I send out compassion and love to this amazing universe;
compassion and love return to me multiplied many times.**

IN THE BEGINNING

This is the place where writers usually summarize what they've said. But you've already read all that. Instead, let's consider how things might be different in your life if meditation were truly a part of it, if you naturally turn to that way of being as your default resource when challenges arise. Here, at the beginning of your journey, it's worthwhile to consider where you can expect to arrive.

We know that people who consistently meditate have a singular ability to cultivate positive emotions, retain emotional stability, and engage in mindful behavior,
—EILEEN LUDERS
postdoctoral research fellow,
UCLA Laboratory of Neuro Imaging

You wake up in the morning refreshed and open to the day's possibilities, but you don't feel the need to hit the ground running. You take a few moments to come fully awake. Sitting on the side of your bed, you take three deep breaths. Maybe you use those moments to clear out the cobwebs of dreams, or you might just reflect at the miracle of another day. Given the uncertainty of life and the complexity of these human bodies, it *is* a miracle.

You give yourself the gift of coming slowly and mindfully into the day. Your morning routines flow simply and efficiently because you're present to them rather than planning ahead, projecting and anticipating, and dropping the soap or throwing away the toothpaste cap because you were thinking about having to face an unpleasant chore.

A period of sitting meditation, even if it's only ten minutes long, is part of your getting ready for the day. You have found a spot near a window and you take in the light and the way the sky looks, even as you enter the centered calm of your meditation. A bird flies past the window and lands in the tree across the street. You see it, and recognize the flash of blue as it turns, but when it disappears in the greenery, you let the thought of it go and you remain in the tranquility of your mind.

When you get up from your meditation, for a few moments at least, things are clearer. You appreciate the way the morning light falls on the rug; the pattern is sharper and there's a flash of memory, where you were when you first saw that rug in the marketplace. . . .

You begin your day in quiet confidence. Waiting for the bus, you keep coming back to exactly where you are. The bus is late and there are more people than usual at the stop. Some of them are clearly annoyed. One woman keeps repeating, "It's never this late. It's going to be too crowded." She runs through a list of people and circumstances to be blamed. You have no need to join her on that detour. A few others contribute to the atmosphere of general discontent. You have better things to do with your mind and your time, but you feel genuine compassion for the distress and for the fact that others don't seem to recognize that distress is optional.

A young woman next to you says she's afraid of being late for work. It'll count against her and they're always looking for reasons to let people go. You decide to say a few words. Surely she can tell them the bus was late, maybe offer to work through lunch or stay few minutes late to make up for it? She looks as distressed at your suggestions as she was in the first place. "But I've got plans," she says and looks away. Priorities. Worry and priorities. You used to worry more, but somehow you don't so much these days. You remember hearing something the Dalai Lama said: "If you can't do anything about it, why waste time worrying? If you can do something, there's no need to worry."

Your priorities seem to sift themselves out more easily. Meditation brings an increase in self-knowledge, so decisions are less arduous. You see where your emotional energy is going and you have some choice in where you spend it. You know where your buttons are and, increasingly, you find yourself able to respond rather than just reacting when somebody pushes them.

Fear gradually diminishes. For one thing, as you feel your own stability increasing, you see other people more clearly. So many negative experiences turn out not to be about you at all. They're other people's anxieties and defenses, and you don't need to get entangled in them. Like a gentle practitioner of a martial art, you can turn aside and let the jabs and provocations slide past. They come from the other person's discontent. It's a shame they feel that way, but once you've checked to see if they've got a legitimate point, you can take the content of the message and let the angry delivery dissolve.

Don't be concerned that you'll become so calm that you'll float through your days like a swan on a lily pond, never getting angry, never feeling hurt or happy, sad or ecstatic. Emotional ups and downs will stay a part of your human experience. The difference is that gradually you notice that you've got a choice as to how you express them. A gap opens between when something strikes you and when you need to respond. You can consider: "That was a hurtful thing he said. But what do I want to happen next? What made him do that? If he's fearful or angry, lashing back will only make things worse." You can take one deep breath and try to answer from your own safe place. "Sorry. I guess that really made you mad. What can I do about it now?"

Of course, there are people who seem to enjoy the drama of confrontation and confusion. It's one way to spend your life. But think of what you might do if you had that energy to use. This is one of the ways meditation increases your capacity to accomplish, to create, to appreciate.

Meditation clears the way for you to emerge fully into your life. You're less a victim of your own compulsions and reactions. In fact, whenever you hear yourself say "I'm the kind of person who. . ." it's worth the time to check that out. Sit with the statement. Consider: Have I always been this way? Is it something I hang onto that isn't really that essential? Let your mind just hold the question lightly. Maybe some insight will occur. Maybe not. After a few minutes, drop the reflection and take up one of your current methods of meditation. You can return to the question after a few minutes of just sitting. Alternating between considering a question, watching where your mind goes, and simple sitting can produce some very worthwhile insights.

If you're troubled by a persistent problem, so that you even find yourself mulling it over at night when you think you should be sleeping, try sitting up and giving it your full attention for a few minutes. Get comfortable, begin your meditation, and then let the problem or situation just occupy your mind for a bit. Don't elaborate on it; just hold it and see where your mind takes it. Then drop it and sit. After a few alternations, know that you've done what you can for now and you can go to sleep. Sometimes it seems as if your cleared mind continues to work on the idea even when you're asleep. The next day may bring a whole different view. If you're still having trouble falling asleep, repeating a mantra can help.

And this is really only the beginning. There is a level of clarity and simplicity, beautiful and rewarding, that becomes accessible to a mind given a chance to experience its own depth and potential. May this little book help you start that journey.

ACKNOWLEDGMENTS

It took a surprising number of people to make this little book come about and I am profoundly grateful to all of them. First of all, to my husband, John, who keeps urging me on. He typeset this book and kept me in encouragement and buckets of tea throughout. To our fabulous daughter, Mariah, and to the infinitely generous Jessie Wood, editors extraordinaire, who rendered it far more readable. To Roger Williams, whose canny publisher's eye saw this full-fledged pullet when it was just an egg, and whose artist's hand produced some of the illustrations. And to son-in-law and gallant savior Joe, whose artistic flexibility enabled him to step in at the last minute and finish my illustrations while I was suffering the consequences of a serious lapse in mindfulness that resulted in a broken arm—of course on the side I hold my pen. Finally my unending gratitude to those teachers of meditation who shared their gifts with me, but most particularly to Sogyal Rinpoche, who has the capacity to make the teachings of the East brilliantly accessible to Western students. It is my great good fortune to be one of them.

ABOUT THE AUTHOR

Marina Bear is enjoying a full and productive life, combining philosophical, business, and educational endeavors with raising a family, writing books, and being active in the art and dance communities. She has been involved for more than 40 years in philosophical traditions in which meditation plays a major role. After many years of teaching ethics, bioethics, logic, and world religions at Vanderbilt University, the University of St. Francis, and Berkeley City College, she now teaches meditation in San Francisco.

Dr. Bear earned her Master's degree in humanities at California State University and a second Master's and Ph.D. in philosophy at Vanderbilt University. She was part of a small team that developed a master plan for a Fortune 500 company's educational division, and was president of a company that worked with the Edinburgh Business School, which offers one of the world's largest MBA programs.

She initiated and taught both remedial and gifted programs in a rural school district, served as co-owner and confectioner at a candy manufacturer and retailer, and recently painted a large mural on a commercial building.

And now you know why she needed to meditate.

She lives in the San Francisco area with her husband of 45 years, author John Bear, and hangs out a lot with their three daughters and their families, including five grandchildren.

Some Other Books by Marina Bear

Meditation and Stress Relief, Worldwise, Inc. San Rafael, 2004 (over 50,000 in print)

Goddesses of the Celestial Gallery, Mandala Publishing, 2006

Maturity, UMI Dissertation Publishing, Ann Arbor, 1993

Not Your Mother's Cookbook: Unusual Recipes for the Adventurous Cook, SLG Books, Berkeley 2002 (with John Bear)

Evening Food, Ten Speed Press, Berkeley 1997 (with Margaret Fox and Christopher Kump)

Luba Gurdjieff: A Memoir with Recipes, Ten Speed Press/Celestial Arts, Berkeley, 1993 (with Luba Gurdjieff), republished by SLG Books, Berkeley

How to Repair Food, Ten Speed Press, Berkeley, 1986 (with John Bear) (over 100,000 in print)

The Something Went Wrong, What Do I Do Now Cookbook, Harcourt Brace Jovanovich, New York, 1970 (with John Bear)

Some Other Books from SLG Books
(www.slgbooks.com)

Mipam: The first Tibetan novel, Lama Yongden

A Tibetan on Tibet, G. A. Combe

The Elegant Taste of Thailand, Pinyo Srisawat and Sisamon Kongpan

Taste of Indonesia: Recipes from the Spice Islands, Helena Soedjak, Ph.D.

Taste of Laos: Lao/Thai Recipes from Dara Restaurant, Daovone Xayavong

Freehand: The Art of Stanley Mouse, Stanley Mouse

Big Yum Yum Book, Robert Crumb

3 1901 05233 5876